The American Kestrel

by: Lisa A. Selner

FIRST EDITION:

(Information address: www.BuffaloAnnie.com)

Edited by: Lee Ann at Book-Editing-Services.com

Illustrations by: Gau Family Studio (www.GauFamilyStudio.com)

Printed in the United States of America

ISBN:

ISBN-13: 978-1540817839

ISBN-10: 1540817830

DEDICATION

This book is dedicated to my nephews, Mason and Connor, sons to my sister, Sarah, and her husband, John. Though I'm missing out on my nephews growing up because I am far from home, they and the rest of my family are always in my thoughts, filled with love and best wishes.

The kestrel teaches control of speed and movement. It teaches patience, as well as quick thinking, survival of self and family, observation, and keen awareness; they teach that size does not constitute strength.

~ Unknown

ABOUT THE AUTHOR

As a wildlife biologist, Lisa A. Selner has been working in wildlife conservation since college. Through her work with various entities throughout the United States, she has embarked on many ventures with a multitude of wildlife species. Some of her most memorable moments have been spent with bears, birds of prey, bison, coyotes, elk, mountain lions, and wild horses! Lisa is also a licensed falconer, or someone who trains birds of prey for hunting. Falconers are highly dedicated individuals who invest a lot of time and energy to working with these birds. In general, falconers have a very positive impact on conservation efforts with regard to birds of prey, and offer a great deal of knowledge about their behavior, ecology, habitat, and natural history.

Photo by Anne Hutton – The author with Cody, a male American kestrel (on the left) and Belle, a female American kestrel (on the right), both used as falconry birds.

ACKNOWLEDGEMENTS

I want to thank the following people for helping me make this book possible:

Lee Ann, a professional editor, for her editing contributions.

Gau Family Studio, for the wonderful work they did with the illustrations.

Anne Hutton, for taking my portrait photo for this book.

Pete Triem, my falconry sponsor while practicing as an apprentice falconer, for encouraging me to write a children's book.

The Peregrine Fund and the American Kestrel Partnership, for allowing me to include their plans for installing an American kestrel nest box.

Finally, I'd like to thank CreateSpace for making the steps towards self-publishing relatively painless.

TABLE OF CONTENTS

Introduction

The American kestrel…

A small slender falcon the size of a robin.

Found in the open, its head sometimes bobbin'.

Often called sparrow hawk but a falcon indeed.

Sparrows aren't always on the menu, we concede.

Habitats with nesting cavities and hunting perches are best.

Anything less would cause much detest.

Once quite numerous in many places,

Habitat loss has minimized their spaces.

Pesticide use also affected them greatly,

But banning their use has helped a bit lately.

The federal Migratory Bird Treaty Act keeps them protected;

The year 1918 was when this law became enacted.

Where do American kestrels live?

In both North and South America the kestrel will reside,

While grandeur and beauty are displayed with great pride.

You'll see them pumping their tails when perched,

Up and down, up and down, their feathers not besmirched.

Known for rapid flight what wondrous airpower,

Recorded at speeds close to 40 miles per hour!

Quite vocal, especially when alarmed or excited,

A loud series of "killy, killy, killy!" calls are recited.

What do American kestrels look like?

The smallest falcon found in North America, no doubt,

But what it lacks in size it makes up for in stout.

Like most falcons that have long pointed wings and long tails,

The kestrel follows suit with such traits that prevail.

Two vertical black lines on each of its cheeks,

Are very appealing; they look like black streaks.

A rufous-colored back and tail are noted as well,

But there are differences too that we must dispel.

The male and female show a difference in plumage,

Almost like autumn and its spectacular foliage.

Unlike other falcon species, this is for sure,

Males have black-banded bluish-gray wings to allure.

As with all birds of prey, the female is bigger.

It must protect its nest and babies with great vigor.

Where do American kestrels hunt?

Grassy areas like hay fields and orchards and pastures will do.

Airports and large parks and powerline right-of-ways too.

Though not unusual to see kestrels in a city,

Some might find this thought quite witty.

Nesting in tree cavities or nest boxes is preferred,

Though nest sites on buildings sit well with this bird.

They also like trees and shrubs and telephone poles to perch,

But it's quite all right if the wood is not made of birch.

What do American kestrels eat?

Diet varies seasonally but is very wide-ranging,

Whatever's available as the seasons keep changing.

From insects to rodents and we'll soon list a few,

Insects: Beetles, butterflies, cicadas, crickets, dragonflies, grasshoppers and moths.

Rodents: Mice, voles, and shrews.

Frogs, lizards, snakes, and small birds are eaten too.

Hunting takes place from a conspicuous perch,

And also while hovering over open fields they search.

A drink is not always sought after a buffet,

All the water they need comes from the moisture of their prey.

Does anything eat American kestrels?

Kestrels may hunt but they are hunted as well,

As part of the food chain Mother Nature does tell.

Owls, hawks, crows, and ravens hunt kestrels too,

Also bobcats, coyotes, raccoons, and skunks to name a few.

Fire ants and various snakes can gobble them in a whisk.

You wouldn't believe your pet dogs and cats could also be a risk.

What is the life history of an American kestrel?

Breeding for kestrels begins in the spring.

Many birds prepare as you'll hear them sing.

Four to six eggs are laid in a rudimentary nest,

Where mainly the female incubates it best.

The male catches most of the food during this time,

Anything he finds is sure to be prime.

The chicks hatch after a month and grow rather fast.

In another months' time they fledge and fly at last.

They will still hang around for a few weeks after that,

But not too long after; they quickly do scat.

What are some of the conservation concerns of American kestrels?

Wildlife surveys have shown population declines.

Loss of habitat is clearly one of many signs.

With farms disappearing and cities on the rise,

It could lead to the kestrel's ultimate demise.

What can you do to help American kestrels?

Nesting cavities are not excavated but rather ready-made.

A kestrel prefers abandoned woodpecker holes or nest boxes manmade.

Nest boxes have helped kestrels where natural cavities are lacking.

If space is available, please help and get cracking!

Do you live by a meadow or a grassy, open field?

You can provide and maintain a nest box to wield.

Get box plans at wildlife offices in your state.

Give them a call and set up a meeting date.

Be sure your habitat has plenty of cover from predators,

Maintenance and monitoring will prevent use by non-native starlings and other competitors.

THE END

NOTE TO PARENTS

American kestrel nest boxes can help kestrels in areas where there are few natural cavities. If you live near suitable habitat, you should consider providing and maintaining a nest box. These habitats include grasslands, hay fields, orchards, and pastures. Nest boxes require regular maintenance and monitoring. Included is a set of directions by the Peregrine Fund and the American Kestrel Partnership. www.peregrinefund.org/american-kestrel

A nest box is easy to build, erect, and maintain.

Good locations for nest boxes include:

- Large trees in the middle or along the edge of a field.
- Barns with an open view for hunting.
- Tall poles surrounded by open fields.
- Open areas where small mammals are common and natural nesting cavities are few.

Tips for a successful nest box:

- Place the nest box 15 to 20 feet from the ground.
- The front of the nest box should be clearly visible from a distance.
- Ensure the nest box is surrounded by a minimum of one acre of open space.
- Orient the nest box so that it faces away from a roadside.
- Place nest boxes at least a half-mile apart if erecting more than one.
- Place nest boxes at least 50 yards from wooded areas.
- Erect nest boxes well before nesting territories are established in the spring.

american
kestrel
partnership

a project of The Peregrine Fund

Build an American Kestrel Nest Box

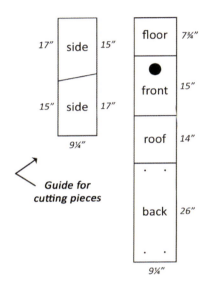

17" side 15"

15" side 17"

9¼"

Guide for cutting pieces

floor 7¾"

front 15"

roof 14"

back 26"

9¼"

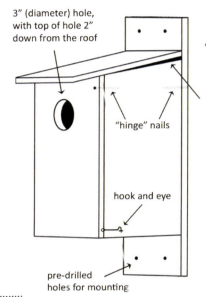

3" (diameter) hole, with top of hole 2" down from the roof

*bevel hinge-side of roof to fit at an angle.

ventilation: 3/8" between roof and side of box

"hinge" nails

hook and eye

pre-drilled holes for mounting

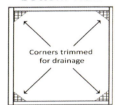

bottom view

Corners trimmed for drainage

*attach floor 1" up from box bottom to protect it from dampness and rotting.

You will need:

- 1" x 10" x 8' untreated cedar or white pine (1" x 10" boards from the store actually measure ¾" x 9¼").
- Two 6d or 8d nails.
- 20-30 1½" wood screws.
- 2" hook and eye closure.
- Coarse wood shavings (not sawdust).
- Four 3" wood screws or lag bolts for mounting.

Visit us! kestrel.peregrinefund.org

Instructions

- Cut lumber using a table saw and entrance hole using a hole saw or jig saw. Pre-drill holes in back if using 3" screws to mount box.
- Assemble box as shown, with wood screws. Nail two 6d or 8d nails parallel at top of opening side, so that it swings open. Attach hook and eye at bottom of hinged side to keep it closed.
- Do not use paint or preservatives.
- Place 2" of wood shavings in the bottom of the box for bedding.
- Mount box at least 6 feet off the ground. Try to space boxes at least ½ mile apart.
- Install nest box by late February, before the breeding season.

THE PEREGRINE FUND

A note on placement: For kestrel parents to find prey around their box, there should be plenty of small rodents or insects nearby. Generally this means low vegetation (lawn grass doesn't count) with a few isolated perches. Avoid wooded areas. Live in a city? No problem! Mount a box on the side of a building. Also be patient, since kestrels don't always move in during the first breeding season.

Isolated trees, wooden poles, barn walls and even low-activity house walls (no doors) are excellent nest box stands. Get permission from your local utility or DOT before mounting boxes on power poles or road signs, and always get permission from public or private property owners before installing boxes.

Safety First! Make sure that nest boxes can be safely accessed for maintenance and monitoring.

66566743R00019

Made in the USA
Charleston, SC
24 January 2017